IT'S TIME TO LEARN ABOUT AFRICAN HUNTING DOGS

It's Time to Learn about African Hunting Dogs

Walter the Educator

Silent King Books
A WhichHead Entertainment Imprint

Copyright © 2025 by Walter the Educator

All rights reserved. No part of this book may be reproduced in any manner whatsoever without written per- mission except in the case of brief quotations embodied in critical articles and reviews.

First Printing, 2024

Disclaimer

This book is a literary work; the story is not about specific persons, locations, situations, and/or circumstances unless mentioned in a historical context. Any resemblance to real persons, locations, situations, and/or circumstances is coincidental. This book is for entertainment and informational purposes only. The author and publisher offer this information without warranties expressed or implied. No matter the grounds, neither the author nor the publisher will be accountable for any losses, injuries, or other damages caused by the reader's use of this book. The use of this book acknowledges an understanding and acceptance of this disclaimer.

It's Time to Learn about African Hunting Dogs is a collectible early learning book by Walter the Educator suitable for all ages belonging to Walter the Educator's Time to Eat Book Series. Collect more books at WaltertheEducator.com

USE THE EXTRA SPACE TO TAKE NOTES AND DOCUMENT YOUR MEMORIES

AFRICAN HUNTING DOGS

Deep in Africa's golden plains,

It's Time to Learn about

African Hunting Dogs

A special dog runs through the rains.

With spots and patches, bold and bright,

They dash so fast, a speedy sight!

African Hunting Dogs, so rare,

Work in teams with love and care.

They never hunt or roam alone,

Their pack's their family, strong and known.

Big round ears help hear so well,

Listening close for sounds to tell.

A rustling bush, a tiny squeak,

They find their food, so quick, so sleek!

They chase together, side by side,

Through grassy fields so far and wide.

They help each other, every one,

Until their hunting job is done.

It's Time to Learn about African Hunting Dogs

Unlike some dogs who bark or growl,

They chatter, chirp, and make a howl.

With whines and yips, they talk all day,

In their own special, secret way.

Their legs are long, their feet are light,

They run so fast, what a sight!

No dog on Earth can match their speed,

They dash with strength and endless need.

But life is tough out in the land,

And humans take what was once grand.

Their homes are shrinking year by year,

And that's a fact we all must hear.

We can help these dogs so true,

By keeping lands where they once grew.

By learning more and spreading cheer,

It's Time to Learn about

African Hunting Dogs

To help them live for many years.

So if you see their spotted fur,

Or hear their voices soft and sure,

Remember they are wild and free,

And need the land, just let them be.

The African Hunting Dog, so grand,

Deserves a place upon this land.

With teamwork strong and hearts so bright,

It's Time to Learn about African Hunting Dogs

They show the world their fearless might!

ABOUT THE CREATOR

Walter the Educator is one of the pseudonyms for Walter Anderson. Formally educated in Chemistry, Business, and Education, he is an educator, an author, a diverse entrepreneur, and he is the son of a disabled war veteran. "Walter the Educator" shares his time between educating and creating. He holds interests and owns several creative projects that entertain, enlighten, enhance, and educate, hoping to inspire and motivate you. Follow, find new works, and stay up to date with Walter the Educator™

at WaltertheEducator.com

www.ingramcontent.com/pod-product-compliance
Lightning Source LLC
LaVergne TN
LVHW012052070526
838201LV00082B/4055